# HAYDN

# Creation

an oratorio for soprano, tenor
& bass soli, SATB & orchestra

*with a separate accompaniment for organ or piano
arranged by Vincent Novello*

Order No: NOV 070158

NOVELLO PUBLISHING LIMITED

# THE CREATION.

## Part the First.

### INTRODUCTION.
### REPRESENTATION OF CHAOS.
### RECITATIVE.

*Raphael.*

In the beginning God created the heaven and the earth; and the earth was without form, and void; and darkness was upon the face of the deep.

### CHORUS.

And the Spirit of God moved upon the face of the waters. And God said, Let there be light: and there was light.

### RECITATIVE.
*Uriel.*

And God saw the light, that it was good: and God divided the light from the darkness.

### AIR.

Now vanish before the holy beams
The gloomy shades of ancient night.
The first of days appears.
Now chaos ends, and order fair prevails.
Affrighted fly hell's spirits black in throngs:
Down they sink in the deep abyss
To endless night.

### CHORUS.

Despairing cursing rage attends their rapid fall.
A new-created world springs up at God's command.

### RECITATIVE.
*Raphael.*

And God made the firmament, and divided the waters which were under the firmament from the waters which were above the firmament: and it was so.
Now furious storms tempestuous rage,
Like chaff, by the winds impelled are the clouds,
By sudden fire the sky is inflamed,
And awful thunders are rolling on high.
Now from the floods in steam ascend reviving showers of rain,
The dreary wasteful hail, the light and flaky snow.

### AIR—*Gabriel.*

The marv'llous work behold amaz'd
The glorious hierarchy of heaven;
And to th' ethereal vaults resound
The praise of God, and of the second day.

### CHORUS.

And to th' ethereal vaults resound
The praise of God, and of the second day.

### RECITATIVE.
*Raphael.*

And God said, Let the waters under the heavens be gathered together to one place, and let the dry land appear: and it was so. And God called the dry land earth, and the gathering of waters called he seas: and God saw that it was good.

### AIR.

Rolling in foaming billows,
Uplifted, roars the boisterous sea.
Mountains and rocks now emerge,
Their tops among the clouds ascend.
Through th' open plains, outstretching wide,
In serpent error rivers flow.
Softly purling, glides on
Through silent vales the limpid brook.

### RECITATIVE.
*Gabriel.*

And God said, Let the earth bring forth grass, the herb yielding seed, and the fruit-tree yielding fruit after his kind, whose seed is in itself, upon the earth: and it was so.

### AIR.

With verdure clad the fields appear,
Delightful to the ravish'd sense;
By flowers sweet and gay
Enhanced is the charming sight.
Here fragrant herbs their odours shed;
Here shoots the healing plant.
With copious fruit the expanded boughs are hung;
In leafy arches twine the shady groves;
O'er lofty hills majestic forests wave.

### RECITATIVE.
*Uriel.*

And the heavenly host proclaimed the third day, praising God, and saying,

### CHORUS.

Awake the harp, the lyre awake,
And let your joyful song resound.
Rejoice in the Lord, the mighty God;
For he both heaven and earth
Has clothed in stately dress.

### RECITATIVE.

#### Uriel.

And **God** said, Let there be lights in the firmament of heaven, to divide the day from the night, and to give the light upon the earth; and let them be for signs, and for seasons, and for days, and for years. He made the stars also.

### RECITATIVE.—(Accompanied.)

In splendour bright is rising now the sun,
And darts his rays; a joyful happy spouse,
A giant proud and glad
To run his measur'd course.
With softer beams, and milder light,
Steps on the silver moon through silent night.
The space immense of th' azure sky
A countless host of radiant orbs adorns.
And the sons of God announced the fourth day,
In song divine, proclaiming thus his power:

### CHORUS.

The heavens are telling the glory of God,
The wonder of his work displays the firmament.

### TRIO.

To day that is coming speaks it the day,
The night that is gone to following night.

### CHORUS.

The heavens are telling the glory of God,
The wonder of his work displays the firmament.

### TRIO.

In all the lands resounds the word,
Never unperceived, ever understood.

### CHORUS.

The heavens are telling the glory of God,
The wonder of his work displays the firmament.

---

## Part the Second.

### RECITATIVE.

#### Gabriel.

And **God** said, Let the waters bring forth abundantly the moving creature that hath life, and fowl that may fly above the earth in the open firmament of heaven.

### AIR.

On mighty pens uplifted soars
The eagle aloft, and cleaves the air,
In swiftest flight, to the blazing sun.
His welcome bids to morn the merry lark,
And cooing calls the tender dove his mate.
From ev'ry bush and grove resound
The nightingale's delightful notes;
No grief affected yet her breast,
Nor to a mournful tale were tun'd
Her soft enchanting lays.

### RECITATIVE.

#### Raphael.

And **God** created great whales, and every living creature that moveth; and God blessed them, saying, Be fruitful all, and multiply.
Ye winged tribes, be multiplied,
And sing on every tree; multiply,
Ye finny tribes, and fill each wat'ry deep;
Be fruitful, grow, and multiply,
And in your God and Lord rejoice.
And the angels struck their immortal harps,
and the wonders of the fifth day sung.

### TRIO.

#### Gabriel.

Most beautiful appear, with verdure young adorn'd,
The gently sloping hills; their narrow sinuous veins
Distil, in crystal drops, the fountain fresh and bright.

#### Uriel.

In lofty circles play, and hover in the air,
The cheerful host of birds; and as they flying whirl
Their glittering plumes are dy'd as rainbows by the sun.

#### Raphael.

See flashing through the deep in thronging swarms
The fish a thousand ways around.
Upheaved from the deep, th' immense Leviathan
Sports on the foaming wave.

#### Gabriel, Uriel, and Raphael.

How many are thy works, O God!
Who may their number tell?

### TRIO AND CHORUS.

The Lord is great, and great his might,
His glory lasts for ever and for evermore.

### RECITATIVE.

#### Raphael.

And **God** said, Let the earth bring forth the living creature after his kind, cattle, and creeping thing, and beast of the earth, after his kind.
Straight opening her fertile womb,
The earth obey'd the word,
And teem'd creatures numberless,
In perfect forms, and fully grown.
Cheerful, roaring, stands the tawny lion. With sudden leap
The flexible tiger appears. The nimble stag
Bears up his branching head. With flying mane,
And fiery look, impatient neighs the noble steed.
The cattle, in herds, already seek their food
On fields and meadows green.
And o'er the ground, as plants, are spread
The fleecy, meek, and bleating flocks.
Unnumber'd as the sands, in swarms arose
The hosts of insects. In long dimension
Creeps, with sinuous trace, the worm.

### AIR.

Now heaven in fullest glory shone;
Earth smil'd in all her rich attire;
The room of air with fowl is filled;
The water swell'd by shoals of fish;
By heavy beasts the ground is trod:
But all the work was not complete;
There wanted yet that wondrous being,
That, grateful, should God's power admire,
With heart and voice his goodness praise.

### RECITATIVE.

#### Uriel.

And God created Man in his own image, in the image of God created he him. Male and female created he them.

He breathed into his nostrils the breath of life, and Man became a living soul.

### AIR.

In native worth and honour clad,
With beauty, courage, strength, adorn'd,
Erect, with front serene, he stands
A man, the lord and king of nature all.
His large and arched brow sublime
Of wisdom deep declares the seat!
And in his eyes with brightness shines
The soul, the breath and image of his God.
With fondness leans upon his breast
The partner for him form'd,
A woman, fair and graceful spouse.
Her softly-smiling virgin looks,
Of flow'ry spring the mirror,
Bespeak him love, and joy, and bliss.

### RECITATIVE.

#### Raphael.

And God saw every thing that he had made, and behold, it was very good. And the heavenly choir, in song divine, thus closed the sixth day.

### CHORUS.

Achieved is the glorious work;
The Lord beholds it, and is pleas'd.
In lofty strains let us rejoice,
Our song let be the praise of God.

### TRIO.

#### Gabriel and Uriel.

On thee each living soul awaits;
From thee, O Lord, all seek their food;
Thou openest thy hand,
And fillest all with good.

#### Raphael.

But when thy face, O Lord, is hid,
With sudden terror they are struck;
Thou tak'st their breath away,
They vanish into dust.
   Gabriel, Uriel, and Raphael.

Thou sendest forth thy breath again,
And life with vigour fresh returns;
Revived earth unfolds new strength
And new delights.

### CHORUS.

Achieved is the glorious work;
Our song let be the praise of God.
Glory to his Name for ever.
He sole on high exalted reigns.
                    Hallelujah!

---

# Part the Third.

INTRODUCTION.—MORNING.

### RECITATIVE.

#### Uriel.

In rosy mantle appears, by music sweet awak'd,
The morning, young and fair.
From heaven's angelic choir
Pure harmony descends on ravish'd earth.
Behold the blissful pair,
Where hand in hand they go: their glowing looks
Express the thanks that swell their grateful hearts.
A louder praise of God their lips
Shall utter soon; then let our voices ring,
United with their song.

### DUET.

#### Adam and Eve.

By thee with bliss, O bounteous Lord,
Both heaven and earth are stor'd.
This world so great, so wonderful.
Thy mighty hand has fram'd.

### CHORUS.

For ever blessed be his power,
His Name be ever magnified.

#### Adam.

Of stars the fairest, pledge of day,
That crown'st the smiling morn;
And thou, bright sun, that cheer'st the world,
Thou eye and soul of all;

### CHORUS.

Proclaim in your extended course
Th' almighty power and praise of God.

#### Eve.

And thou that rul'st the silent night
And all ye starry hosts,
Ev'rywhere spread wide his praise
In choral songs about.

#### Adam.

Ye mighty elements, by his power
Your ceaseless changes make;
Ye dusky mists, and dewy streams,
That rise and fall thro' th' air;

### CHORUS.

Resound the praise of God our Lord.
Great his name, and great his might.

### Eve.

Ye purling fountains, tune his praise;
And wave your tops, ye pines.
Ye plants, exhale, ye flowers, breathe
To him your balmy scent.

### Adam.

Ye that on mountains stately tread,
And ye that lowly creep;
Ye birds that sing at heaven's gate,
And ye that swim the stream;

### Eve and Adam.

Ye creatures all, extol the Lord;

### CHORUS.

Ye creatures all, extol the Lord;
Him celebrate, him magnify.

### Eve and Adam.

Ye valleys, hills, and shady woods,
Made vocal by our song,
From morn till eve you shall repeat
Our grateful hymns of praise.

### CHORUS.

Hail! bounteous Lord! Almighty, hail!
Thy word call'd forth this wondrous frame,
The heavens and earth thy power adore;
We praise thee now and evermore.

### RECITATIVE.

### Adam.

Our duty we have now perform'd,
In offering up to God our thanks.
Now follow me, dear partner of my life,
Thy guide I'll be; and every step
Pours new delights into our breasts,
Shows wonders everywhere.
Then mayst thou feel and know the high
Of bliss the Lord allotted us,     [degree
And with devoted heart His bounties celebrate.
Come, follow me, thy guide I'll be.

### Eve.

O thou for whom I am, my help, my shield,
My all, thy will is law to me;
So God our Lord ordains; and from obedience
Grows my pride and happiness.

### DUET.

### Adam and Eve.

*Adam.*    Graceful consort, at thy side
        Softly fly the golden hours;
        Ev'ry moment brings new rapture,
        Ev'ry care is lull'd to rest.

*Eve.*    Spouse adored, at thy side
        Purest joys o'erflow the heart;
        Life and all I have is thine;
        My reward thy love shall be.

*Both.* The dew-dropping morn, O how she
        quickens all!
        The coolness of even, O how she all
        restores!
        How grateful is of fruits the savour
        sweet!
        How pleasing is of fragrant bloom the
        smell!
        But, without thee, what is to me
        The morning dew, the breath of even,
        The sav'ry fruit, the fragrant bloom?
          With thee is every joy enhanced,
          With thee delight is ever new,·
          With thee is life incessant bliss,
          Thine, thine it all shall be.

### RECITATIVE.

### Uriel.

O happy pair! and happy still might be
If not misled by false conceit.
Ye strive at more than granted is;
And more desire to know, than know ye should.

### CHORUS.

Sing the Lord, ye voices all,
    Magnify his name thro' all creation,
    Celebrate his power and glory,
Let his name resound on high.
Praise the Lord.  Utter thanks.
Jehovah's praise for ever shall endure. Amen.

# THE CREATION.

## PART I,

**No. 1.**   INTRODUCTION.—REPRESENTATION OF CHAOS.

**No. 2.**

RECITATIVE (BASS).—"IN THE BEGINNING."

URIEL (TENOR).

And God saw the light, that it was good: and God di-vi-ded the light from the dark-ness.

No. 3.　　　Air (Tenor).—"NOW VANISH BEFORE THE HOLY BEAMS."

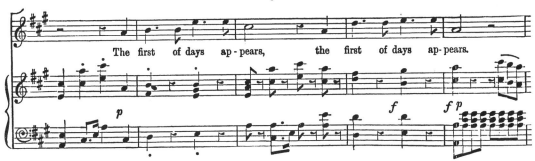

The first of days ap-pears, the first of days ap-pears.

Now cha-os ends, and or - der, and

or - der fair pre - vails, Now cha-os ends,

now cha - os ends, and or - der fair pre - vails, and or - der

fair pre - vails.

**3**

Af-fright - ed fly hell's spi-rits black    in throngs :    Down    they

sink    in    the    deep    a - byss    To    end - less    night,

Down    they    sink    in    the    deep . . .    a -

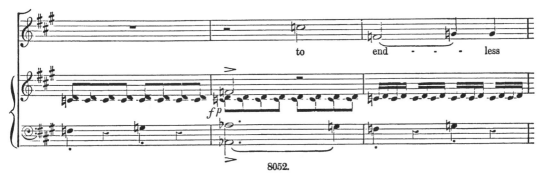

- byss    To    end - less    night,

to    end - - - less

8

-mand, a new-cre-a-ted world, a new-cre-a-ted

-mand, a new-cre-a-ted world, a new-cre-a-ted

- mand, a new-cre-a-ted world, a new-cre-a-ted

- mand, a new-cre-a-ted world, a new-cre-a-ted

world springs up, springs up at God's com - mand.

world springs up, springs up at God's com - mand. URIEL.

world springs up, springs up at God's com - mand. Af -

world springs up, springs up at God's com - mand.

- fright - - ed fly hell's spi - rits black in throngs: Down they sink in the deep a -

**No. 4.**      RECITATIVE (BASS).—"AND GOD MADE THE FIRMAMENT."

Like chaff, by the winds im- pell'd are the clouds,

By sud - den fire the sky is in -

- flam'd,

And aw- ful thunders are roll-ing on high

Now from the floods    in steam as - cend    re - vi - ving show - ers of    rain,

The drea - ry waste - ful    hail,

the light and fla - ky snow.

No. 5.  SOLO (SOPRANO) AND CHORUS.—"THE MARV'LLOUS WORK."

18

8052.

No. 6.   RECITATIVE (BASS).—"AND GOD SAID, LET THE WATERS."

No. 7.   AIR (BASS).—"ROLLING IN FOAMING BILLOWS."

**1** RAPHAEL

Roll - - - ing in foam - - ing bil - lows, Up -

- lift - - - ed, roars the boist - 'rous sea,

Roll - ing in foam - ing bil - lows, Up - lift - ed, up -

lift - - ed, roars the boist - 'rous sea, up - lift - ed

roars the boist'rous sea. Mountains and rocks now e -

- merge, Their tops a - mong the clouds as - cend, their tops a -

- mong the clouds as - cend, Mountains and rocks now e - merge, Their

tops a-mong the clouds as - cend, their tops a - mong the clouds as - cend, a - mong the

er - ror riv - ers flow, . . . . . . . . riv - ers

flow. . . . . . . .

Soft - - ly purl - - ing, glides

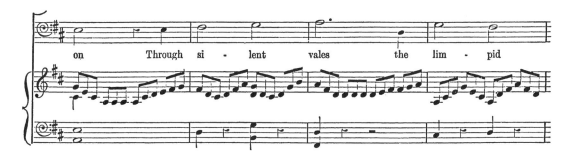

on Through si - lent vales the lim - pid

brook, Soft - - ly purl - ing,

glides . . . . . on Through si - lent vales the

**4**

lim - pid brook, Soft - - ly purl - - ing,

glides on Through si - lent vales the

lim - pid brook, Soft - ly

purl - ing, glides . . . . . on Through

si - - lent vales . . the lim - pid brook,

through si - lent vales the lim - pid brook.

**No. 8.**     Recitative (Soprano).—"AND GOD SAID, LET THE EARTH."

GABRIEL.

And God said, Let the earth bring forth grass, the herb yield-ing seed, and the fruit-tree yield-ing fruit af - ter his kind, whose seed is in it - self, up - on the earth: and it was so.

No. 9.                    AIR (SOPRANO).—"WITH VERDURE CLAD."                    GABRIEL.

here shoots the heal - ing plant, . . . . the heal - ing

plant, . . . . . here shoots the heal - ing plant.

**2**

With co - pious fruit th' ex - pand - ed boughs are

hung; In leaf - y arch - es twine the sha - dy

groves; O'er loft-y hills ma-jes - tic for - ests wave, ma-jes-tic for-ests

**3**

wave. With ver - dure clad the

'fields ap-pear, De-light-ful to . . the rav-ish'd sense; By flow - ers sweet and gay

En - han-ced is the charming sight, en - han - - - ced

**4**

is the charming sight. Here fra - grant herbs their

o - dours shed; Here shoots the heal - ing plant, . . . . .

. . . . . . . here shoots the heal - - ing plant,

*p*

**5** Here fra - grant herbs their o - dours shed; Here shoots the heal - ing plant, . . . .

. . . . the heal - ing plant, . . . . the heal - ing plant, . . . . . here

*fz*          *pp*

shoots . . the heal - - ing plant.

*f*

*No.* 10.    Recitative (Tenor).—"AND THE HEAVENLY HOST."

*No.* 11.    Chorus.—"AWAKE THE HARP."

*No. 12.* RECITATIVE (TENOR).—"AND GOD SAID, LET THERE BE LIGHTS."

**No. 18.**   Recitative (Tenor).—" IN SPLENDOUR BRIGHT."

To run his measur'd course. With soft-er beams, and mild-er .. light, Steps on the sil-ver moon through si - - - lent night. The space immense of th'a-zure sky A countless host of ra-diant orbs a-dorns. And the sons of God an-nounced the fourth day, In song di-vine, pro-claim-ing thus his pow'r:

No. 14.    Chorus.—"THE HEAVENS ARE TELLING."

D

**2**

fol - low-ing night.

fol - low -ing night.

fol - low-ing night.

The hea - vens are tell - ing the glo - ry of God, The

The hea - vens are tell - ing the glo - ry of God,

The hea - vens are tell - ing the glo - ry of God, The won - der,

The hea - vens are tell - ing the glo - ry of God, The won - der, the

*f*

won-der of his work, the won-der of his work dis - plays the fir - ma - ment,

The won-der of his work, dis - plays, dis - plays the fir - ma - ment,

the won-der of his work dis - plays, dis - plays the fir - ma - ment,

won-der of his work, the won-der of his work dis - plays the fir - ma - ment,

*fz*

the won-der of his work dis-plays the fir-ma-ment.

the won-der of his work dis-plays, dis-plays the fir-ma-ment.

the won-der of his work dis-plays, dis-plays the fir-ma-ment.

the won-der of his work dis-plays the fir-ma-ment.

GABRIEL.

In all the lands re-

URIEL.

In all the lands re-sounds the word,

RAPHAEL.

In all the lands re-sounds the..

-sounds the word, Nev-er un-per-ceiv-ed, ev-er un-der-stood, ev-er,

Nev-er un-per-ceiv-ed, ev-er un-der-stood, ev-er,

word, Nev-er un-per-ceiv-ed, ev-er un-der-stood, ev-er,

ev - er,   ev - - er un - der - stood,

ev - er,   ev - - er un - der - stood,

ev - er,   ev - - er un - der - stood,

In all the lands re - sounds the

In all the lands re - sounds the word,

In all the lands re - sounds the word,

word,   Nev - er un - per - ceiv - ed,   ev - er un - der - stood,   ev - er,

Nev - er un - per - ceiv - ed,   ev - er un - der - stood,   ev - er,

Nev - er un - per - ceiv - ed,   ev - er un - der - stood,   ev - er,

ev - er, ev - - er un - der - stood, ev - er, ev - er, ev - -

ev - er, ev - - er un - der - stood, ev - er, ev - er, ev - -

ev - er, ev - - er un - der-stood, ev - er, ev - er, ev - -

*f*

*Voices alone.*

*a tempo.*     *Più Allegro.*    **3**

- er, . . ev - - er un - der - stood.

*a tempo.*

- er, ev - - er un - der - stood.

*a tempo.*

- er, ev - - er un - - der - stood.

*Più Allegro.* *f*

The hea - vens are tell - ing the

*f*

The hea - vens are tell - ing the

*f*

The hea - vens are tell - ing the glo - ry of

*f*

The hea - vens are tell - ing the glo - ry of

*Più Allegro.* ♩= 144.

*p a tempo.*     *f*

52

5

END OF PART I

# PART II.

**No. 15.**  Recitative (Soprano).—"AND GOD SAID, LET THE WATERS."

**No. 16.**  Air (Soprano).—"ON MIGHTY PENS."

**2**

GABRIEL.

On might - y

pens up - lift - ed soars The ea - gle a-loft, the ea - gle a - loft, and cleaves the

air, In swift - est flight, in.. swift - est flight, to the bla - zing

sun,      to the bla - zing   sun.

*fz*      *f*      *p*

His   wel - come bids    to morn the mer -ry

lark,      his   wel - come bids    to morn the mer - ry

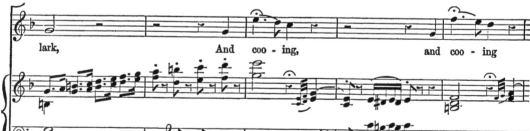

lark,      And   coo - ing,      and coo - ing

**3**

*tr  tr*      *tr  tr*

calls the ten - der dove   his mate,    calls the ten - der dove   his mate,

and coo - ing, and coo - ing calls the ten - der dove his mate,

calls the ten - - der dove . . his mate. On might - - y

pens up - lift - ed soars The ea - gle a - loft, His

wel - come bids to morn the merry lark, And coo - ing,

and coo - ing calls the ten - der dove his mate,

calls the ten - der dove    his mate                and    coo - ing, and coo - ing

calls the ten - der dove    his mate,        calls    the    ten - - - der    dove . . .    his

mate,        the    ten - - - - - - - - - - - - - - - - - der

dove    his    mate.

From ev - 'ry bush . . and grove re -
sound The night - in - gale's de - light - - - - ful notes;
No . . grief af -
- fect - ed yet her breast, Nor . . to a mourn-ful tale were
tun'd Her soft, . . her soft enchanting

E

her soft en-chanting lays, her soft

en - chant - ing lays, her

soft en-chanting lays, her . . soft en-chanting lays.

**No. 17.** RECITATIVE (BASS).—" AND GOD CREATED GREAT WHALES.

No. 18       Recitative (Bass).—"AND THE ANGELS."

RAPHAEL.

And the an - gels struck their im - mor - tal harps, and the

won - ders, the won - ders of the fifth day sung.

**No. 19.**  Trio.—"MOST BEAUTIFUL APPEAR."

Gabriel.

Most beau - ti - ful ap - pear, with ver - dure young a -

- dorn'd, The gen - tly slo - ping hills, the gen - tly slo - ping hills;

their nar - row sinuous veins Dis - til, in crys-tal drops, the

fountain, the foun - tain fresh . . and bright, Their nar-row sin-uous

veins Dis - til, in cry- stal drops, the foun - tain fresh and bright.

URIEL.

In loft - y cir-cles play, and hov-er in the air, The

cheer - ful host of birds, the cheer-ful host of birds; and

as they fly-ing whirl, Their glit-'tring plumes are dyed as rain-bows, as

rain - bows by . . the sun, And as they fly - ing

whirl, Their glit-t'ring plumes are dyed as rain - bows by . . the

RAPHAEL.

See

sun.

flash-ing thro' the deep in thronging swarms The fish a thou - sand ways . . a-round, a

thou - sand ways a - round. Up-heav - ed

from the deep, th'immense Le - vi - a-than

Sports on the

GABRIEL.

How

foam - - ing wave, sports on the foam - - ing, foam - ing

fz

ma - ny are thy works, O God, how ma - ny are thy works, O God! Who

URIEL.

How ma - ny are thy works, O God, how ma - ny are thy works, O God!

wave. How ma - ny are thy works, O God! Who may their number

fz fz fz fz fz

may their number tell, who may their number tell, who may . . their number tell?

Who may their number tell, who may . . their number tell, their number tell?

tell, who may their number tell, who may their num - ber tell?

fz fz

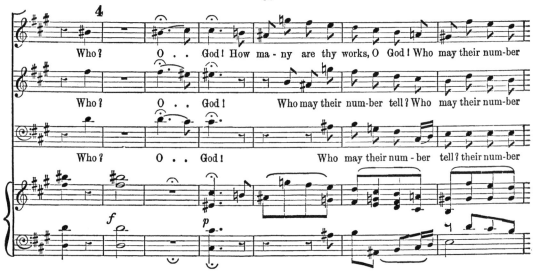

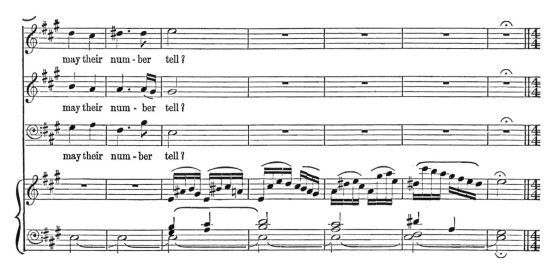

No. 20.     TRIO AND CHORUS.—"THE LORD IS GREAT."

ev - - er and for ev - - - er -

ev - - er and for ev - - - er -

ev - - er and for ev - - - er

**1**

- more, his glo - - - - - - - - - - - - ry . .

- more, his glo - - - ry, his glo - ry

- more, his glo - - - ry, his glo - ry

**Chorus.**
**Soprano.**

The Lord is great, . . . and great his might, . . the Lord is great, . . .

**Alto.**

The Lord is great, . . . and great his might, the Lord is

**Tenor.**

The Lord is great, . . . and great his might, . . the Lord is

**Bass.**

The Lord is great, . . . and great his might, . . his glo - ry

*f*

No. 21. Recitative (Bass).—"AND GOD SAID, LET THE EARTH BRING FORTH."

And God said, Let the earth bring forth the liv - ing crea-ture af-ter his kind, cat - tle, and creep-ing thing, and beast of the earth, af-ter his kind.

No. 22. Recitative (Bass).—"STRAIGHT OPENING."

Straight o - pen-ing her fer-tile womb,

The earth o-bey'd the word, And teem'd crea-tures num-ber - less, In perfect forms, and ful - ly grown.

Cheerful, roaring,

stands the tawny li-on.

With sudden leap The flexible ti-ger appears.

The nimble stag Bears

up his branch-ing head.

With flying mane, And fie-ry look, im-patient neighs the noble steed.

*Andante.*

*Andante.* ♪ = 120.

The

cattle, in herds, al - rea - dy seek their food On fields and meadows green.

And o'er the ground, as plants, are spread The flee - cy,

meek, and bleat - ing flocks. Unnumber'd as the sands, in swarms a -

*Adagio.*

rose The hosts of in - sects. *Adagio.* ♪ = 88.

*a tempo.*

In long di - mension Creeps, with sin - uous trace, the worm.

*fz* *p a tempo.*

fill'd ;        The wa - - ter swell'd      by     shoals . . of

fish ;        By  heav - y beasts   the   ground  is  trod,

by  heav - y beasts   the   ground  is   trod :

But all the

work was not complete,   but all the work was not complete ;       There  want - ed

yet that wondrous be - ing, That, grate - ful, should God's pow'r ad - mire,

With heart and voice his good - ness

praise. But all the work was not com - plete ; There wanted

yet that wondrous be - ing, That, grate - ful, should God's pow'r . . ad - mire, With

heart and voice his good - ness praise, That,

grate - ful, should God's pow'r ad - mire, With heart and voice, with

heart, . . . . . with heart and voice . . . his

good - ness praise, with heart and voice, with

heart and voice his . . good - ness praise.

No. 24.    RECITATIVE (TENOR).—"AND GOD CREATED MAN."

URIEL.

And God cre - a - ted Man    in   his own im - age,    in   the im - age of

God cre - a - ted he him.    Male and fe-male cre-a - ted he them.    He brea - thed

in - to his nos-trils the breath of life,    and Man    be - came a liv-ing soul.

No. 25.    AIR (TENOR).—"IN NATIVE WORTH."

Andante. ♩ = 88.

URIEL.

In na - tive worth and hon - our clad, With beau - ty, cour - age,

strength, a-dorn'd, E - rect, with front se - rene, he stands A man, the

lord and king of na - ture all.

His large and arch - ed brow sub-lime

Of wis - dom deep de - clares the seat! And

in his eyes with bright - ness shines The soul, the

breath and im - - age of his God,

And in his eyes with bright - - ness shines The soul, the breath and im - - age of . . . his God.

**3**

bliss,                    Her soft - ly - smi - ling vir - gin looks,                    **Of**

flow'r - y spring . . . the mir - ror,                    Be - speak . .

him love, . .                    love, . . . and

joy, . . . and bliss,                    be - speak him

love,          and joy, . . . . . . and bliss. . . . .

**No. 26.** Recitative (Bass).—"AND GOD SAW EVERY THING THAT HE HAD MADE."

**No. 27.** Chorus.—"ACHIEVED IS THE GLORIOUS WORK."

No. 27A.  TRIO.—"ON THEE EACH LIVING SOUL AWAITS."

soul awaits; From thee, O Lord, all seek their food; Thou o - pen-est thy hand, And fill - est, and

soul awaits; From thee, O Lord, all seek their food; Thou o - pen-est thy hand, And fill - est, and

fill - - est all . . with good.

fill - - est all . . with good.

RAPHAEL.

But when thy face, O

Lord, is hid, With sud - den ter - ror they are

struck; Thou tak'st their

breath a-way, They van-ish in-to dust, Thou

tak'st their breath a-way, They van-ish in-to

GABRIEL.

Thou send-est forth thy breath a-gain,

URIEL.

Thou send-est forth thy breath a-gain,

dust: Thou send-est forth thy breath a-gain,

**1**

And life with vig-our fresh re-turns; Re-

And life.. with vig-our fresh.. re-turns; Re-vi-ved earth un-

And life with vig-our fresh re-turns; Re-vi-ved earth un-

-vi - ved earth un - folds    new    strength And new de - lights,                Re - -

- folds    new    strength And new de- lights,  and new de - lights,                Re - -

- folds    new    strength And new de- lights,  and new de - lights,    Re - vi - ved earth un -

- vi - ved earth un - folds    new    strength And new de - lights,

- vi - ved earth un - folds    new    strength And new de - lights,

- folds    new    strength And new de - lights,    new    strength and new de -

**2**

· · ·    new strength and new de-lights,         And    life    with vigour fresh returns ;   Re -

new strength and new de-lights,  And  life    with vigour fresh returns ; Re - vi - ved earth un-

- lights,    new strength and new de-lights,    And  life    with vigour fresh returns ;  Re - vi - ved earth un-

No. 27B.   SECOND CHORUS.—"ACHIEVED IS THE GLORIOUS WORK."

END OF PART II.

# PART III.

**No. 28.** Introduction (Morning) and Recitative.—"IN ROSY MANTLE APPEARS."

H

- pears, by mu-sic sweet a - wak'd, The morning, young and fair.

From heav'n's an - gel - ic choir Pure har - mo-ny des-

- cends on 'ra - vish'd earth. Be-hold the bliss- ful

pair, Where hand in hand they go : their glowing looks Express the thanks that

swell their grateful hearts. A louder praise of God their lips Shall ut-ter soon ; *Più moto.*

then let our voices ring, U - ni -ted with their song.

## DUET AND CHORUS.—"BY THEE WITH BLISS."

won-derful, Thy might - - y hand . . . has fram'd, thy might-y

won-derful, Thy might - - y hand has fram'd, thy might-y

his Name be ev - er mag - ni-fied, be

his Name be ev - er mag - ni-fied, be

his Name be ev - er mag - ni-fied, be

his Name be ev - er mag - ni-fied, be

hand has fram'd, thy might-y hand has fram'd. . . . .

hand . . has fram'd, thy might-y hand has fram'd. . . . .

mag - ni - fied, be mag - ni - fied. . . . .

mag - ni - fied, be mag - ni - fied. . . . .

mag - ni - fied, be mag - ni - fied. . . . .

mag - ni - fied, be mag - ni - fied. . . . .

night And all ye star-ry hosts, Spread

wide, and ev'-ry-where spread wide his praise In chor - al songs . . a-

- bout, Spread wide, . . and ev'-ry-where his praise

ADAM.

In chor - al songs . . a - bout. Ye might-y el - e-ments,

by his pow'r Your cease-less chan - ges make, your cease-less chan - ges

make; Ye, ye dusk -y mists, and dew -y steams, That rise and fall thro' th' air, that rise and fall thro' th' air;

**7**

Eve.
Re-sound the praise of God our Lord, re-sound the

Adam.
Re-sound the praise of God our Lord, re-sound the

Chorus.
Soprano.
*f*
Re-sound the praise of God our Lord,

Alto.
*f*
Re-sound the praise of God our Lord,

Tenor.
*f*
Re-sound the praise of God our Lord,

Bass.
*f*
Re-sound the praise of God our Lord,

**8**

great his might.

great his might.

great his might.

great his might.

great his might.

great his might.

*p*

EVE. *p*

Ye purl - - ing foun - tains, tune his praise;.. And

wave your tops, ye pines... Ye

*cres.*

*p*

plants, ex - hale, ye flow - ers, breathe, breathe To him . . your

balm - y scent. Ye plants, ex - hale, ye

flow - ers, breathe, breathe To him . . your balm - y scent.

**9**

ADAM.

Ye

that on mountains stately tread, And ye that low-ly creep;

**11** EVE. Ye ADAM. Ye

val - leys, hills, and sha - dy woods, . . Made vo - cal by our song, . .

val - leys, hills, and sha - dy woods, Made vo - cal by our song,

**12**

From morn till eve you

From morn till eve you

shall re - peat Our grate - ful hymns . . of praise, From

shall re - peat Our grate - ful hymns of praise,

morn . . . . . . . . . . . . . till eve you shall re-

From morn till eve you shall re-peat, from morn till eve you

peat Our grate - ful, our grate - - - - ful hymns . . of

shall re-peat Our grate - ful, our grate - - - - ful hymns . . of

praise.

praise.

**13**

Chorus.

Hail! boun - teous Lord! Al - might - - - y,

Hail! boun - teous Lord! Al - might - - - y,

Hail! boun - teous Lord! Al - might - - - y,

Hail! boun - teous Lord! Al - might - - - y,

cres.

16

**17**

The heav'ns and earth thy pow'r a - dore; We praise thee

The heav'ns and earth thy pow'r a - dore; We praise thee

The heav'ns and earth thy pow'r a - dore, thy pow'r a - dore; We praise thee

The heav'ns and earth thy pow'r a - dore, thy pow'r a - dore; We praise thee

now and ev - - - er - more, and ev - - er - more, and

now and ev - - - er - more, and ev - - er - more, and

now and ev - - - er - more, and ev - - er - more, and

now and ev - - - er - more, and ev - - er - more, and

ev - - er - more.

ev - - er - more.

ev - - er - more.

ev - - er - more.

No. 30. RECITATIVE (ADAM AND EVE).—"OUR DUTY WE HAVE NOW PERFORMED."

with de-vo-ted heart His bounties cel-e-brate. Come, come, fol-low me,

fol-low me, thy guide I'll be. O thou for whom I am, my

help, my shield, My all, . . thy will is law to me:

So . . God our Lord or-dains; and from o-be-dience, and from o-

be-dience Grows my pride . . . . . and hap-pi-ness.

No. 31.   DUET (ADAM AND EVE).—"GRACEFUL CONSORT."

con-sort, Ev-'ry moment brings new rap-ture, Ev-'ry care is lull'd.. to rest.

1 EVE.

Spouse . . . . a - dor -ed, at thy side . . Pu - rest

joys o'er-flow the heart; Life and all I have, all I

have is thine; My re - ward, .. my re - ward thy love .. shall

be, .. Spouse a - dor - ed, Life and all I have, all I

have is thine; My re - ward thy love .. shall be, Spouse a - dor - ed, at thy side .. Purest

Grace-ful con - sort, at thy side, .. at thy side ..

joys .. o'erflow the heart; Life and all .. I have is thine; My re -

Soft - ly fly .. the gold-en hours; Ev - 'ry mo - ment brings new

- ward, my re -ward thy love shall be, .. Spouse a - dor - ed, Life and

rap - ture, Ev - 'ry care is lull'd to rest, Grace-ful con - sort, Ev - 'ry

*fz*   *p*

all I have, all I have is thine; My re - ward thy love .. shall be, ..

mo-ment brings new rap - ture, Ev - 'ry care is lull'd .. to rest, .. Grace-ful

*fz*   *p*   *fz*   *p*

Spouse a - dor - ed, My re - ward, .. my re - ward thy love .. shall

con - sort, grace - ful con - sort, Ev - 'ry care, .. ev' - ry care is lull'd .. to

**2** *Allegro.*

be.

rest.     The dew-drop-ping morn,     O how she quickens all!

*Allegro.* ♩ = 88.

The cool-ness of ev'n,     O how she

all restores!

How grate - ful

How pleas - ing is .. of

is .. of fruits the sa-vour sweet!

fragrant bloom the smell! But, with-out thee, but, with-out thee,

But, with-out thee, but, with-out thee, but, with-out

what is to me the breath of ev'n,

thee, what is to me The morn-ing dew,

the frag - rant bloom? With

The sa - v'ry fruit, With

thee, with thee is ev-'ry joy en-han-ced, With thee, with

thee de-light is ev-er new, With thee, with

thee .. is life . . in-ces-sant bliss, Thine, thine,

**4**

thine it all . . shall be, With

K

The cool-ness of e'en, O how she all restores!

How grate - ful is . . of

How pleas - ing is . . of

fruits the sa-vour sweet!

fragrant bloom the smell! But, with-out thee, but, with-out thee,

But, without thee, but, without thee, but, without

what is to me                    the breath of ev'n,

thee, what is to me          The morning dew,

**7**

the frag-rant bloom?

The sa-v'ry fruit,

With thee, with thee is ev-'ry joy en-han-ced,          With

With thee, with thee is ev-'ry joy en-han-ced,          With

**8**

thee, with thee de-light is ev-er new,          With thee,

thee, with thee de-light is ev-er new,          With thee,

with thee    is    life . . . . in - ces - sant bliss,    Thine,

with thee    is    life . . . . in - ces - sant bliss,    Thine,

thine,    thine it    all . . . . .    shall    be,

thine,    thine it    all . . . . .    shall    be,

**9**

With thee,    with thee,    with thee . .

With thee,    with thee,    with thee . .

. . . . . . . is life,    is life . . in - ces - sant bliss, Thine,    thine it

. . . . . . . is life,    is life    in - ces - sant bliss, Thine,    thine it

all . . shall be, With thee is life in-ces-sant bliss,

all . . shall be, With thee is life in-ces-sant bliss,

*dolce.*

Thine, . . . . thine . . . . it all shall

Thine, . . . . thine . . . it all shall

be, it all . . . . . shall be. . . .

be, . . . it all shall be. . . .

*f*

**No. 32.**     RECITATIVE (TENOR).—"O HAPPY PAIR!"

O happy pair! and happy still might be    If not misled    by false conceit. Ye strive at

more than grant-ed is;    And more de-sire to know,    than know ye should.

**No. 33.**     CHORUS.—"SING THE LORD, YE VOICES ALL."

Sing the Lord, ye voi-ces all,    Mag-ni-fy    his Name thro' all cre-a-tion,

Sing the Lord, ye voi-ces all,    Mag-ni-fy    his Name thro' all cre-a-tion,

Sing the Lord, ye voi-ces all,    Mag-ni-fy    his Name thro' all cre-a-tion,

Sing the Lord, ye voi-ces all,    Mag-ni-fy    his Name thro' all cre-a-tion,

Printed and bound in Great Britain by
Caligraving Limited Thetford Norfolk

THE END

# CONTENTS.